How to be a...

SKATEBOARDING CHAMPION

James Nixon

W

FRANKLIN WATTS

LONDON • SYDNEY

First published in 2015 by
Franklin Watts
338 Euston Road
London NW1 3BH

Franklin Watts Australia
Level 17/207 Kent Street
Sydney NSW 2000

© 2015 Franklin Watts

ISBN 978 1 4451 3620 2
Library eBook ISBN 978 1 4451 3622 6

Dewey classification number: 796

In preparation of this book, all due care has been exercised with regard to the advice, activities and techniques depicted. The publishers regret that they can accept no liability for any loss or injury sustained. When learning a new activity, it is important to get expert tuition and to follow a manufacturer's instructions for any equipment you are using.

A CIP catalogue record for this publication is available from the British Library.

Planning and production by Discovery Books Limited
Managing Editor: Paul Humphrey
Editor: James Nixon
Design: sprout.uk.com
Picture research: James Nixon

Printed in China

Franklin Watts is a division of Hachette Children's Books, an Hachette UK Company.
www.hachette.co.uk

Photo acknowledgements: Cover photo: (Shutterstock: A Einsiedler)
Alamy: pp. 4 bottom (Star Stock), 9 top (Paul Matzner), 11 top (ZUMA Press, Inc), 13 bottom (ZUMA Press, Inc), 15 top (epa european pressphoto agency b.v.), 17 bottom (ZUMA Press, Inc), 20 bottom (ZUMA Press, Inc), 22 top (GoodSportHD.com), 23 top (ZUMA Press, Inc), 23 bottom (WENN Ltd), 24 (ZUMA Press, Inc), 25 top and bottom (ZUMA Press, Inc), 26 (ZUMA Press, Inc), 27 bottom (CTK), 29 bottom (ZUMA Press, Inc). Bobby Humphrey: pp. 7 middle, 11 bottom, 15 bottom, 22 bottom. Shutterstock: pp. 4 top (homydesign), 5 (homydesign), 6 top (HomeArt), 6 bottom (Underworld), 8 left (lzf), 8 right (homydesign), 9 middle (lzf), 9 bottom (A Einsiedler), 10 top (Maksim Shirkov), 10 bottom (lzf), 12 top and bottom (ARENA Creative), 13 top (Jose Gil), 14 top (Joakim Lloyd Raboff), 14 bottom (Ian Woolcock), 15 middle (Frenzel), 16 left (Photographee.eu), 16 right (ARENA Creative), 17 top (Cylonphoto), 17 middle (homydesign), 18 left (homydesign), 18 right (Charles Knox), 19 top (homydesign), 19 bottom (Pio3), 20 top (homydesign), 21 top (homydesign), 21 botttom (A Einsiedler), 27 top (s_bukley), 28 top (MJTH), 28 bottom (Troy Kellogg), 29 top (Nejron Photo). Vertical Urge: p. 7 top. Wikimedia: p. 7 bottom (Ybes03).

Every attempt has been made to clear copyright. Should there be any inadvertent omission please apply to the publisher for rectification.

CONTENTS

The skaters featured in this book sometimes skate without their safety gear on. However, we advise that you should always wear safety gear when performing tricks (see page 7).

All words in **bold** can be found in the glossary on page 31

WHY SKATE?

Skateboarding is one of the most popular sports in the world. For most people, cruising around on a board and trying out tricks is just a great way to have fun. Others take skateboarding to the extreme. These skaters can pull off spectacular stunts and routines and become sporting superstars.

LEARNING NEW MOVES

The great thing about skateboarding is that there are hundreds and hundreds of tricks, and no matter how good you get, there are always new moves to learn. You can take skateboarding to whatever level you choose. However, you must be patient. Professionals who skate for a living have spent years training and have special talent.

Skateboarding is a test of skill and courage.

TOP DOG

Tony Hawk from the USA is probably the most famous skateboarder of all time. Hawk's speciality was **vert** riding. In the '80s and '90s he developed many new and insane-looking tricks and was crowned Vert World Champion 12 years in a row! In 1999, just before he retired, he became the first ever rider to land a '900' trick – two and a half spins in mid-air.

A BIT OF HISTORY

The idea of skateboarding began in the late 1950s when surfers in California decided they wanted to surf the streets. Skateboarding really took off in the late 1970s when the technology improved. Suddenly, boards were smoother, easier to turn and a lot more fun to ride. The first concrete **skate parks** also started to be built.

Skateboarders took advantage of the new boards and started inventing new tricks. In the 1980s and '90s, skaters continued to do things on a board that no one had thought possible. The popularity of skateboarding surged again. By the end of the 1990s, competitions could be seen on TV and skateboarders became top athletes.

PARK, STREET AND VERT

The three main types of skateboarding competition are 'park', 'street' and 'vert'. In park and street contests, riders use obstacles found in a skate park or town, such as kerbs and rails. Skaters in vert competitions show off mind-blowing stunts on a huge U-shaped ramp with vertical walls. Riders are judged on their tricks and how stylishly they pull them off.

A skater shows off his tricks in a skate park.

GEAR GUIDE

The board is obviously the most important part of a skateboarder's kit. A board gets lots of bumps and knocks. Make sure you know the names of all the board's parts because you will have to repair and replace stuff when it wears out.

Deck – A deck is built from seven layers of maple wood glued and pressed together. The wood is shaped with a tail and nose that curve upwards. Cool graphics are painted under the bottom sheet of maple.

Grip tape – This is like black sandpaper glued to the top of the deck. The rough surface helps you grip the board with your shoes and perform tricks more easily.

Tail

Nose

Trucks – The trucks connect the wheels to the deck. They give you the ability to turn and control your skateboard while you roll.

Kingpin – By tightening or loosening the nut on this bolt, you can adjust the speed at which the trucks turn.

BUYING A BOARD

When you buy your first board, make sure you get good advice from a quality skate shop. A cheap board might seem like a good idea, but it won't last as long. It is worth buying parts separately so that you can spend a little extra on the important parts such as the wheels and trucks.

When choosing a deck, you need to consider your height. You can buy kids' decks that are smaller than the average 18-cm width. Try out different sizes to see which you find most comfortable.

Skate shops have a wide choice of decks to buy.

Wearing safety gear will help to prevent you getting injured.

Skate shoes are designed especially for skateboarding.

SAFETY GEAR

All skaters should wear hard pads and helmets to protect themselves. Helmets come in many styles. A helmet should fit on your head snugly. If it slides around when you move, it's not tight enough.

Falling is part of learning to skate, but knee and elbow pads will take a lot of the impact. Pads should be tight, but not so tight that they stop your blood flowing.

SKATE SHOES

A proper pair of skate shoes will last a lot longer than a regular pair of trainers. Skate shoes are designed to have sturdy soles, which will not wear away on the board's grip tape. They are also built with more padding and support around the ankles and heels, to help you avoid injuries such as **sprains**.

BASIC SKILLS

Skateboarding takes time to learn – even the basics. To start with, you need to learn how to hop on the board, push off, turn and stop, until it becomes so natural that you don't notice what you are doing.

REGULAR OR GOOFY?

To step on the board, put your leading foot just behind the front truck, with your toes facing forwards. If you prefer to lead with your left foot you are 'regular'. Riding with your right foot out in front of you is called 'goofy'. Either way is fine, so choose whichever is more comfortable for you. Top skaters can switch between regular and goofy with ease.

A goofy-footed rider pushes off.

PUSHING OFF

Pushing the board along is pretty simple. With your weight over a bent front leg, use the back leg to push off the ground. You will need four solid pushes to get a decent amount of speed. Now you can get both feet on the deck by putting your back foot between the rear truck and tail.

You can perform a 'tic-tac' to keep your speed up. Raise the front of the board up by leaning on the tail, and then shift the board sideways with your front foot before putting the wheels back down. Quickly repeat this move, but this time, shift the board the other way, and you will gather up speed.

TURNING AND STOPPING

Skateboarding wouldn't be much fun if you could only travel in a straight line. Turning, known as carving, is done by leaning your heels or toes in the direction you want to turn. The more pressure you apply with your heels or toes, the tighter you will turn. Use your arms to help you balance.

The easiest way to stop is called the foot drag. While coasting on your front foot, hover your back foot above the ground. Steadily add pressure to the ground with your foot to slow down gradually.

A tail skid can also bring you to a stop. Move your back foot to the back of the board and force your weight back so that the board and heel scrape the ground (right).

A skater pushes his heels down to carve the board.

RECORD BREAKERS

Brazilian skateboarder Bob Burnquist (left) born in 1976 has had an astonishing career. The **X Games** is the Olympic Games of skateboarding and Burnquist has won more medals at them than any other rider in history. His 27 X Games medals include 12 gold, seven silver and eight bronze!

THE OLLIE

Most skateboard tricks are not possible unless you know how to do the 'ollie'. An ollie is when you hop up into the air with your feet seemingly stuck to the board. It is quite simply the most important trick to learn.

Once you've mastered the ollie you will be able to leap over things.

HOW TO DO IT

Just because the ollie is the first trick to learn does not make it easy. Take your time to perfect it and be patient.

1 Crouch down on your board with your front foot behind the front truck. Your back foot should be at the very back, overhanging your heel so that your toes are in the middle of the tail.

2 Kick down your back foot as hard as you can and take the weight off your front leg to let the board point upwards.

3 As soon as you feel your foot hitting the floor, jump back up and forwards. It's all about timing.

4 As you pop up, drag your front foot along the grip tape towards the nose. This helps you lift the board up into the air.

5 Guide the board with your feet to keep it level in mid-air, and remember to bend your knees when you land to absorb the shock.

It is best to attempt the ollie standing still at first. Once that feels comfortable try an ollie while you are moving. The more you practise the higher you can jump.

At the same time as jumping to ollie, scrape the side of your front foot up the grip tape.

Nyjah Huston (left) from California, USA, started skating when he was 5 years old. At the age of only 11 he became the youngest ever X Games competitor! By the age of 19 Huston had won more prize money than any other skater in history. He continues to push the limits of what is possible on a skateboard. At the 2014 X Games Huston scored 95.00, the highest ever points total in the history of the Street event.

THE NOLLIE

The nollie is the ollie in reverse. Instead of slapping the tail down before you jump, you kick down the nose. Nollies are a lot harder because you are using your back foot to guide the board into the air.

A WORLD OF TRICKS

Mastering the ollie enters you into a whole new world of tricks. A frontside ollie is where you swing your chest forwards with your arms so that you land facing the opposite way. A backside ollie is where your back is thrown around to turn you through 180 degrees.

A 'pop shove-it' is where you spin the board around 180 degrees beneath your feet. As you hit the tail down to ollie, just shove the board to the side at the same time to get it turning. The trick is then to catch the board with your front foot to land once the board has turned around.

As the board turns around during a 'pop shove-it', stay over it ready to land.

FLIP TRICKS

A flip trick is when the board is flipped over in mid-air. Flip tricks always look impressive, and there is no better feeling than when you land one.

THE KICKFLIP

The kickflip is usually the first flip trick skaters learn. It is done by flicking the board with your front foot, so that it spins upside down and back around. As you perform an ollie, scrape your front foot up the deck towards the heel-side. Then kick the heel-side of the nose with your toes to get the board turning.

Keep your eyes on the board as it levels out and aim to land your feet over the truck bolts. The higher you can ollie the more time you have to flip and catch the board, so get your ollies perfected first. To begin with, if you want to feel safer, you can practise your kickflips on grass while holding on to a fence or railing.

On a kickflip, start the deck turning with your front toes.

Keep your eyes on your board as it rotates beneath you.

HEEL FLIP

Heel flips are like kickflips except that your heel flicks the board over. Ollie up and slide your front foot diagonally up towards the toe-side of the nose. Kick the side of the deck with your heel to flip the board over. You need to learn how hard to flick so that the board spins the right amount.

MIXING TRICKS

Skateboarding is all about keeping it fresh. This means doing tricks in a different way or mixing up tricks to test yourself and impress your friends.

The frontside flip is a frontside ollie and a kickflip combined. The same goes for the backside flip. The 'varial flip' is a combination of a kickflip and a pop shove-it. The board rotates from nose to tail and flips over from top to bottom in one quick trick. A '360 flip' is even more insane. The board rotates through a full circle (360 degrees) at the same time as being flipped.

There are many different flip tricks to learn.

TOP DOG

Lacey Baker (left) from California, USA, is one of the best female skaters in the world. Baker is a goofy-footed rider who specialises in street tricks. The 22-year-old started skating seriously at the age of 11 and won her first Street gold medal at the 2014 X Games in Austin, Texas, USA. Baker says her proudest moment in her life was when she landed a kickflip for the first time!

AT THE SKATE PARK

The best place to practise your skateboarding tricks is at your local skate park. These are built with ramps and curves so that you can flow without having to take your feet off to push. You can build up enough speed to tackle obstacles such as rails and jumps.

Skate parks contain bowls that are like shallow, empty swimming pools with ramps on all sides.

Mini ramps are usually good for beginners, but they do vary in size.

RAMPS AND PIPES

Skate parks contain a mixture of ramps, from simple launch ramps to large **halfpipes**. They all help you get into the air so that you can do flips and **grab** tricks.

A mini ramp has a flat bottom in the middle with a small ramp at each end. Skaters can **transition** from one ramp to the other without stopping. Halfpipes look like a pipe cut in half and have much higher ramps. When you drop into a halfpipe you go so fast that you can catch air the other side. A quarter pipe is a single, steep ramp. Running along the top of most ramps are steel tubes called **coping**.

Nineteen-year-old Pedro Barros (left) from Brazil is the world's best park skater right now. Since 2010 he has won five X Games gold medals in the Park event. Barros is a master on the halfpipe, but it is the bowl where he can really destroy the competition. He can put together moves that are beyond most people's imagination. Barros practises on a huge skate park at his home in Brazil, which is open to the public.

STREET FURNITURE

Many skate parks have street features such as stairs, railings and benches. The top skaters can ollie up to slide on these obstacles and pull off amazing tricks. Blocks and flatbars are great skate park objects for beginners that are learning to slide. Blocks have metal edges for sliding. Flatbars are square rails that are low to the ground.

The ledges on blocks are ideal for sliding tricks.

PARK SAFETY

Skate parks can get very busy so always be aware of what is going on around you. Crashing into other skaters will not make you any friends. Don't be embarrassed to learn how to skate on the smaller features – that's what they are there for. Never skate obstacles outside your limits.

You must learn how to fall safely on the ramps. If you feel yourself starting to fall, step off the board. As your foot hits the ground, drop to your knees and fall on the pads. Don't stick out your arms to break a fall or you could break them instead!

When you fall on a ramp, slide safely to a stop with your knees tucked in together.

RIDING RAMPS

Transitions are the curves on any kind of ramp. Skaters will tell you how much fun it is to ride transitions, but it takes practice. Here are some tips to make you look stylish on the ramps and keep you in full control.

DROPPING IN

Dropping in to a ramp is harder than it looks. In fact it is one of the scariest things you will learn on a skateboard. Once you lean forward to drop, don't think about falling. If you hesitate and lean backwards you are going to fall off.

At the top of a ramp, hold the tail firmly against the coping with your back foot (below). Move your front foot on to the truck bolts at the nose and take the plunge! You need to lean forward and stay with the board the whole way. It's all about balance.

PUMPING AND TURNING

You can use an action called pumping to build up speed on transitions. As you roll up to the top of a transition, straighten your legs out. As you begin to roll back down, crouch and lean in the direction you are heading.

Kick turns come in handy when you don't have enough speed to reach the coping. As you ride up the ramp, lift your front foot up slightly to lift the nose upwards and guide it in the direction you want to go while you **pivot** on the back truck.

As you roll down a transition, crouch to build up speed.

16

STALLS

Another way to ride from coping to coping is to stall at the lip of the ramp, before riding back down. These neat lip tricks are moves you just have to learn. On a basic stall, shift your weight on to the nose or tail so that you can rest on the coping for a moment or two.

By approaching at a slight angle and lifting the front wheels to go above the lip you can also rest the trucks on the coping. This is called an axle-stall.

FAKIE

Riding backwards in your normal stance is called riding fakie. To do the 'rock-fakie' trick, lift the nose over the coping by pressing your back foot down and then shift your weight forwards to stall the middle of the board on the coping. Now shift your weight back to unlock the front wheel and roll back down the ramp fakie.

Push your foot down to stall the nose or tail on the coping.

Be careful if you attempt a rock fakie. It is easy to get stuck on the coping and fall.

RECORD BREAKERS

Extreme skateboarder Danny Way from Oregon, USA, has broken many skateboarding records. Back in 2005 he used a giant ramp to jump over the Great Wall of China! On his second try he landed the jump perfectly. In 2006, Way made the largest drop-in to a halfpipe ever when he **free-fell 8.53 metres from the top of the Hard Rock Hotel in Las Vegas (left).**

BUILD RAMPS NOT BOMBS

GRINDS AND SLIDES

Grinds and slides are the ultimate tricks to test your balance and board control. Plus, they look awesome. Grinding is travelling along an object on the board's trucks. A slide is when you travel along a ledge on the underside of your deck.

MAKING IT GRIND

You can grind your board on pretty much anything – metal rails, concrete steps, even wooden benches. But grinds are tough moves, so as ever, start with something small and work your way up.

The '50-50 grind' is the easiest to learn. This is where both trucks glide along a rail at the same time. You need to be able to ollie higher than the obstacle you are grinding. You also need enough speed so that when you land on the ledge you grind instead of stall. Your body weight must be centred over the board. As you reach the end of the grind, pop the nose up to help you drop off the edge.

MIXING IT UP

The top skaters can pull off an amazing variety of grinds. During a '5-0 grind' a skater glides on the back truck and keeps the nose in the air. The opposite of the 5-0 is the 'nose grind'.

A 'crooked grind' is a nose grind at an angle.

You can '50-50 grind' on the coping of a ramp or bowl.

NOSE AND TRUCK GRINDS

As you ollie up to nose grind, start with your front foot nearer the nose of the board. Then you can push the nose down in mid-air to land on the front truck. A 'crooked grind' is similar, but you land the nose down on the rail and grind at a 45-degree angle.

On 'smith' and 'feeble' grinds, you grind the back truck while the front truck hangs off to the side of the rail.

A skater balances himself with his arms during a smith grind.

BOARDSLIDES

When learning slides and grinds you need to be prepared to fall a lot. It takes a while to work out how to shift your weight correctly. You can slide on the nose, tail or middle of the board. This is how you do a simple backside boardslide.

1 Roll towards a flatbar at good speed with your heels and back facing the bar.

2 Use the ollie and throw your shoulders around slightly to land sideways on to the bar.

3 It's important to keep the deck level and face forwards in the direction you are sliding.

4 Keep your knees bent and arms out to help you balance.

5 As you pop off the end of the bar, twist your body and the board back into the riding position.

6 Roll away with a smile on your face.

As you get near to the end of the flatbar, get ready to turn back into the riding position.

AERIAL TRICKS

Aerials are where skateboarding tricks get bigger and higher. These stunts are usually performed on halfpipes and often combine spins with grabs of the board. They can be pulled off by ollieing just as the front wheels reach the lip of the ramp.

GETTING AIR

Leaping into the air with your skateboard is a real buzz. The simplest trick is to twist through 180 degrees (a half-turn) before landing back on the ramp. This is how it's done:

1 Ride with good speed up the ramp at a slight angle towards the direction you are going to spin.

2 Make sure your knees are tucked in and, as the board starts to rise over the coping, twist your body and swing your arms to pull yourself around.

3 Keep over the board as you guide it around with your feet and compress your body to absorb the landing.

Master your ollies before attempting a 180 aerial.

4 On landing, lean forward to ride back down the ramp.

An aerial where the rider spins in one full rotation is called a '360'. It is most commonly performed from the fakie position. This means the rider will land facing forwards when they land back down on the ramp.

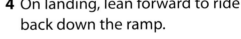

Tom Schaar

RECORD BREAKERS

A 1,080-degree spin, or three full turns, was long thought to be impossible. However, in 2012, Tom Schaar (see page 29) from the USA, did it, at the age of just 12! Schaar rode in fakie, turned backside and grabbed the toe-side of the board between his feet, to complete the three spins. Schaar said 'It was the hardest trick I've ever done, but it was easier than I thought.'

GRAB IT

Using a hand to hold the board to stop it floating away during an aerial is called a grab. Grabs look super-stylish and there are endless variations of grabs to learn. Here are some of the most popular.

Nosegrab – Grab the nose with your front hand.

Tail grab – Reach behind and grab the tail with your back hand.

Cannonball – Crouch to grab the nose and tail with your front and back hand.

Indy – Grab the side of the board in which your toes are pointing, while turning backside. Grip the board between your legs using your back hand.

Melon – Hold the back of the board between your feet with your front hand.

Roast beef – Trail your back hand between your legs to grab the back of the board.

A skater pulls off the 'indy' grab.

Slob-air – Riding frontside up the ramp, grab the toe-side of the board and launch into the air.

Judo – Take your front foot off the board and kick it forwards, while pulling the board backwards.

Rocket air – Grab the nose with both hands and at the same time place both feet on the tail!

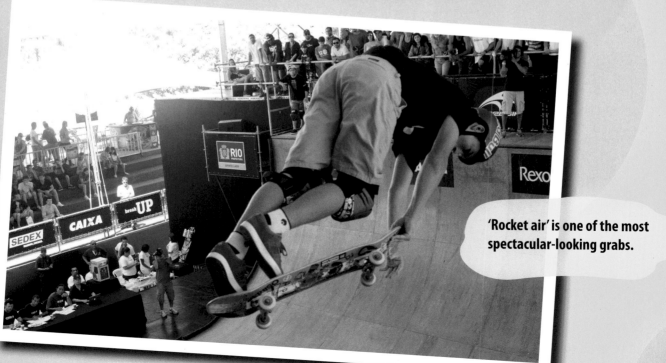

'Rocket air' is one of the most spectacular-looking grabs.

VERT RIDING

Vert ramps look huge and scary. The name vert comes from the vertical walls of the halfpipe, which can be up to five metres high. The steepness of vert ramps means riders can reach amazing speeds and fly high in the air. The top skaters pull off dangerous stunts that are well beyond regular skaters.

PUMPING A VERT

Even the most basic skills such as stalls and turns feel amazing on massive vert ramps. Imagine grinding on the coping of a four-metre vert ramp at top speed. To get a taste of vert, it's a good idea to start by practising your pumping. This means taking big sweeps back and forth between the coping, both forwards and fakie.

To carve on the vert's transition, lean into the ramp with your chest as you turn. Keep leaning to push yourself around until you are at the highest point.

Vert legend Bob Burnquist can pull off some crazy shapes and tricks in mid-air.

HEAD OVER HEELS

Professional vert skaters carry out some truly jaw-dropping and death-defying moves. As well as huge spins, the best riders can land front and back flips. This is when the rider launches off the vert ramp and flies head over heels with the board. The skater has to land backwards, making it even more difficult. Tricks like these have to be learned in the gym by launching off a ramp and landing in a **foam pit**.

TOP DOG

Pierre-Luc Gagnon (right) from Canada is one of the most successful vert riders in history. Gagnon fell in love with the sport at a young age when he was bought a skateboard for his 8th birthday. After lots of hard work he turned professional at 16, and within a year he was invited to compete in the X Games.

Since 2000, his amazing mixture of tricks has won him 19 medals at the X Games, including eight golds in the Vert competition. Gagnon says 'Skateboarding is not just something I do, it's a way of life. It's my way to be creative and original.'

THE X GAMES

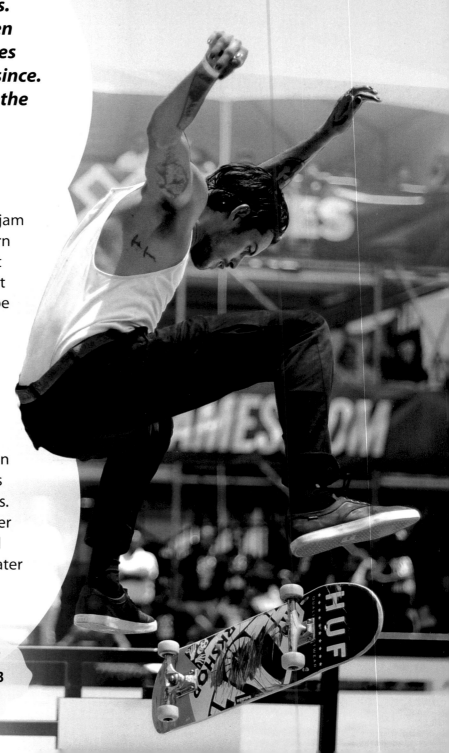

The X Games is the biggest event for professional skateboarders. The Games began in 1995 when it was called the Extreme Games and has been held every year since. Skaters take it in turns to wow the crowds and go for gold.

JAMMING

Skaters at the X Games compete in a jam format, which means each rider in turn has to finish a routine of tricks in a set amount of time. In the Park and Street competitions a skater's session may be 10 or 15 minutes long. The obstacles are built to make the course look like a skate park or part of a street. In Vert events, the riders may have as little as 45 seconds to show off their moves on the ramp.

A panel of judges score each rider's run from 1 to 100. Landing all of the tricks you attempt will score you high marks. The score also depends on the number and variety of tricks, how difficult and original they are and how well the skater used the course.

Street skater Dylan Rieder of the USA competes in the 2013 X Games in Los Angeles.

The Big Air ramps are daunting for the riders but make for spectacular viewing.

BIG AIR

There is a fourth skateboarding competition for skaters at the X Games called Big Air, and it's the craziest of the lot. It is not a timed event. The riders take it in turns to bomb down a 25-metre 'megaramp', which then shoots them into the air across a giant 21-metre gap.

The rider pulls off a stunt in mid-air before landing in an 8-metre high halfpipe. At the other end of the halfpipe, the rider then has to pull off a second amazing aerial trick to finish. It's a spectacular but risky event and crashes are common.

MAKING IT TO THE TOP

X Games competitors achieve their dream through many years of practice, working gradually towards incredibly hard tricks and moves. If you are talented enough, and do well in local competitions, you may be able to get some **sponsorship**. Filming videos of your skateboarding skills and shooting photos to send to magazines will spread the word of your skating skills even further. The top skaters are sponsored by skateboard and clothing manufacturers and earn enough money to travel the world to compete.

RECORD BREAKERS

At the 2000 X Games, Charles 'Bucky' Lasek (left) from Maryland, USA, scored 98.50 for his vert routine, the highest ever score in skateboarding history.

STORY OF A CHAMPION

RYAN SHECKLER

In 2003, aged 13, Ryan Sheckler became the youngest person ever to win an X Games gold medal when he won the Park title. It made Sheckler one of the most famous athletes in the world.

A CHILD SENSATION

Sheckler was born in California in 1989 and started rolling on a skateboard on his driveway before he was 2! By the time he was 4 he could do ollies, and he learned his first kickflip when he was 6. At 7 he got a mini ramp for the back garden and started practising every day.

Sheckler's rare talent began to reveal itself. Between 1999 and 2002 Sheckler, with the help of his mother, travelled all over the USA to enter competitions. Then in 2003 he had his incredible **debut** season as a professional, as his sponsors toured him all across the world. In his X Games-winning performance, Sheckler was the only skater to land every trick he attempted.

Ryan Sheckler on his way to winning Street gold at the 2010 X Games.

A CELEBRITY LIFE

Sheckler's fame continued to grow. In 2005 he was named Action Sports Tour's (AST) Athlete of the Year and dominated the AST's **Dew Tour** in the Park event, winning the Championship three years running between 2005 and 2007. In 2007, Sheckler was even given his own TV show in a series called *Life of Ryan*, which followed Sheckler in his day-to-day life.

Sheckler has since concentrated on street skating. He won gold again in the Street events at the 2008 and 2010 X Games, and continues to be successful. In 2012 and 2013 Sheckler was victorious in the Dew Tour Street competition.

At the 2010 Teen Choice Awards, Sheckler was given the prize of best 'Male Action Sports Star'.

TOP DOG

Leticia Bufoni (right) is one of the best street riders in women's skateboarding. Since 2010 she has been Street World Cup champion four times in a row. In 2013 she won her second Street gold at the X Games. The 21-year-old was born in São Paulo, Brazil, and decided to take up skateboarding when she saw her neighbour riding a board. Bufoni's grandmother bought her a board and took her to the skate park every day. Bufoni has now moved to the USA to skate full-time.

KEEPING FIT

Skateboarders need more than just talent – they also need to know how to look after their bodies. Skateboarding takes loads of energy and is a heavy work-out for your muscles and tendons. Your body needs to be up to the job, so that you can keep doing tricks all day.

Knee stretch

WARMING UP

Before a session it's important to warm up and stretch. This will help to reduce the chance of you getting injured. Here are some good stretches you can do.

Back stretch – Sit down with your legs in front of you on the floor. Then, with a straight back, try to touch your toes with both hands.

Knee stretch – Stand upright, stand on one leg, and lift the other foot up behind you with a bent knee. Gently pull to stretch your knee and thigh muscles.

Calf stretch – Stand on tiptoes on the edge of a step with your heels overhanging. Raise yourself up and down on your tiptoes. Repeat several times.

INJURIES

Even if you are cautious, skateboarding injuries are common, especially to your wrists and ankles if you fall on them. You can buy wrist and ankle supports that can help you prevent and heal a sprain.

Falling awkwardly can cause injury to your foot or ankle.

If you do sprain a joint, put ice on it as soon as you can to help the swelling go down. Arnica cream is a useful product if you have bruised yourself. Spread it on the affected part of your body to lessen the pain.

FOOD AND DRINK

Skateboarders need to keep drinking throughout the day as it is easy to become **dehydrated** when you sweat. Your performance will suffer if you dehydrate so take a large bottle of water to the skate park with you.

A healthy diet will also make you fitter and stronger. Before a competition or big session it is a good idea to load your body up with **carbohydrates**. These can be found in potatoes, rice and pasta. The ideal foods for your lunchbox are high-energy snacks, such as fruit, cereal bars or jam sandwiches.

Replace the fluid you sweat out by drinking lots of water.

TOP DOG

US teenager Tom Schaar (right) is one of skateboarding's biggest superstars. It seems unreal, but in 2012, Schaar was invited to take part in the X Games at the age of just 12. Competing against many of his **idols**, Schaar was able to finish sixth in the Big Air contest. Known for his incredible spins, Schaar went on to win silver in 2013 and gold in 2014 at the age of 14. The boy wonder has a big future ahead of him!

FIND OUT MORE

BOOKS

Adrenalin Rush: Skateboarding,
Jackson Teller, (Franklin Watts 2013)

Freestyle Skateboarding Tricks: Flat Ground, Rails and Transitions,
Sean D'Arcy, (A & C Black Publishers 2010)

No Limits: Skateboarding,
Rob Bowden, (Franklin Watts 2010)

Skateboarding Skills: Everything a New Rider Needs to Know,
Ryan Stutt, (Firefly Books 2014)

Skateboarding: Landing the Basic Tricks,
Ryan Stutt, (A & C Black Publishers 2009)

WEBSITES

www.wikihow.com/ Category:Skateboarding
A series of 'How to…' guides for skateboarders

www.redbull.com/uk/en/skateboarding
Find out the latest news in the world of skateboarding

www.how2skate.com/tricktips.htm
A huge selection of skateboard trick tips

http://skateboard.about.com/od/tricktips/ tp/New_Skaters_Guide.htm
A guide for skateboarding beginners

www.skateboardtricksforbeginners.com/ tag/skateboarding-tips
More skateboarding advice and tips for beginners

www.skateparkfinder.co.uk
Find a skate park near you

Website disclaimer: Note to parents and teachers: Every effort has been made by the Publishers to ensure that these websites are suitable for children, that they are of the highest educational value, and that they contain no inappropriate or offensive material. However, because of the nature of the Internet, it is impossible to guarantee that the contents of these sites will not be altered. We strongly advise that Internet access is supervised by a responsible adult.

GLOSSARY

aerial a skateboarding trick performed high in the air, such as a spin or flip

carbohydrates a group of foods that can be broken down to release energy in the body

coping the protective metal edge running along the top of a ramp

debut a person's first appearance in an event

dehydrate lose a large amount of water

Dew Tour An extreme sports' championship held and televised in the USA with competitions for street-style skaters

foam pit a soft landing area designed with a bed of foam blocks, used by skaters to reduce the risk of injury when they are practising extreme stunts

free-fell dropped from a height under the force of gravity only

grab a skateboarding trick where the skater grabs hold of the board in mid-air

halfpipe a U-shaped ramp, which skaters can ride up and down to perform a variety of tricks

idol a person you admire strongly

pivot turn around a central point

routine a sequence of actions that make up a performance

skate park an area built with ramps and other obstacles for skateboarding

sponsorship funding for a sportsperson's costs in return for advertising

sprain twist a joint, such as an ankle or wrist, to cause pain and swelling

tendon a cord of strong tissue attaching muscle to a bone

transition skate along the curve on a ramp

vert vert describes a large ramp with vertical walls at the top of the transitions

X Games a sports event where competitors compete for gold, silver and bronze medals in a variety of extreme sports

INDEX